Haro
Anto

In 19~~ he won the David Cohen British L~~
awarded for a lifetime's achievement in literature. In 1996
he was given the Laurence Olivier Award for a lifetime's
achievement in theatre. In 2002 he was made a Companion
of Honour for services to literature. In 2005 he was
awarded the Nobel Prize for Literature and, in the same
year, the Wilfred Owen Award for Poetry and the Franz
Kafka Award (Prague). In 2006 he was awarded the Europe
Theatre Prize and, in 2007, the highest French honour, the
Légion d'honneur. He died in December 2008.

HAROLD PINTER

The Caretaker

faber and faber

First published in 1960 by Eyre Methuen
Revised edition 1962

Published in 1991 by Faber and Faber Limited
3 Queen Square London WC1N 3AU
Reset in 2000

Photoset by Parker Typesetting Service, Leicester
Printed in Great Britain by CPI Bookmarque, Croydon, CR0 4TD

© Theatre Promotions Limited, 1960

A CIP record for this book is available
from the British Library.

ISBN 978-0-571-16079-2

The Caretaker was first presented by the Arts Theatre Club in association with Michael Codron and David Hall at the Arts Theatre, London, on 27 April 1960.

On 30 May 1960, the play was presented by Michael Codron and David Hall at the Duchess Theatre, London, with the following cast:

MICK, *a man in his late twenties* — Alan Bates
ASTON, *a man in his early thirties* — Peter Woodthorpe
DAVIES, *an old man* — Donald Pleasence

Directed by Donald McWhinnie

On 2 March 1972, a revival of the play was presented at the Mermaid Theatre, London, with the following cast:

MICK — John Hurt
ASTON — Jeremy Kemp
DAVIES — Leonard Rossiter

Directed by Christopher Morahan

The play was produced at the Shaw Theatre, London, in January 1976, with the following cast:

MICK — Simon Rouse
ASTON — Roger Lloyd Pack
DAVIES — Fulton Mackay

Directed by Kevin Billington

The Caretaker was revived in a National Theatre production in November 1980, and was broadcast by the BBC in March 1981, produced by Alan Shallcross. The cast was as follows:

MICK	Jonathan Pryce
ASTON	Kenneth Cranham
DAVIES	Warren Mitchell

Directed by Kenneth Ives

The Caretaker was revived by Triumph Proscenium Productions at the Comedy Theatre on 20 June 1991. The cast was as follows:

MICK	Peter Howitt
ASTON	Colin Firth
DAVIES	Donald Pleasence

Directed by Harold Pinter

The action of the play takes place in a house in west London.

ACT I A night in winter
ACT II A few seconds later
ACT III A fortnight later

A room. A window in the back wall, the bottom half covered by a sack. An iron bed along the left wall. Above it a small cupboard, paint buckets, boxes containing nuts, screws, etc. More boxes, vases, by the side of the bed. A door, up right. To the right of the window, a mound: a kitchen sink, a stepladder, a coal bucket, a lawn-mower, a shopping trolley, boxes, sideboard drawers. Under this mound an iron bed. In front of it a gas stove. On the gas stove a statue of Buddha. Down right, a fireplace. Around it a couple of suitcases, a rolled carpet, a blow-lamp, a wooden chair on its side, boxes, a number of ornaments, a clothes horse, a few short planks of wood, a small electric fire and a very old electric toaster. Below this a pile of old newspapers. Under ASTON's *bed by the left wall, is an electrolux, which is not seen till used. A bucket hangs from the ceiling.*

Act One

MICK *is alone in the room, sitting on the bed. He wears a leather jacket.*

Silence.

He slowly looks about the room looking at each object in turn. He looks up at the ceiling, and stares at the bucket. Ceasing, he sits quite still, expressionless, looking out front.

Silence for thirty seconds.

A door bangs. Muffled voices are heard.

MICK *turns his head. He stands, moves silently to the door, goes out, and closes the door quietly.*

Silence.

Voices are heard again. They draw nearer, and stop. The door opens. ASTON *and* DAVIES *enter,* ASTON *first,* DAVIES *following, shambling, breathing heavily.*

ASTON *wears an old tweed overcoat, and under it a thin shabby dark-blue pinstripe suit, single-breasted, with a pullover and faded shirt and tie.* DAVIES *wears a worn brown overcoat, shapeless trousers, a waistcoat, vest, no shirt, and sandals.* ASTON *puts the key in his pocket and closes the door.* DAVIES *looks about the room.*

I

ASTON

Sit down.

DAVIES

Thanks. (*Looking about*) Uuh ...

ASTON

Just a minute.

ASTON *looks around for a chair, sees one lying on its side by the rolled carpet at the fireplace, and starts to get it out.*

DAVIES

Sit down? Huh ... I haven't had a good sit down ... I haven't had a proper sit down ... well, I couldn't tell you ...

ASTON

(*placing the chair*) Here you are.

DAVIES

Ten minutes off for tea-break in the middle of the night in that place and I couldn't find a seat, not one. All them Greeks had it, Poles, Greeks, Blacks, the lot of them, all them aliens had it. And they had me working there ... they had me working ...

ASTON *sits on the bed, takes out a tobacco tin and papers, and begins to roll himself a cigarette.* DAVIES *watches him.*

All them Blacks had it, Blacks, Greeks, Poles, the lot of them, that's what, doing me out of a seat, treating me like dirt. When he come at me tonight I told him.

Pause.

ASTON

Take a seat.

DAVIES

Yes, but what I got to do first, you see, what I got to do, I got to loosen myself up, you see what I mean? I could have got done in down there.

DAVIES *exclaims loudly, punches downward with closed fist, turns his back to* ASTON *and stares at the wall.*

Pause. ASTON *lights a cigarette.*

ASTON

You want to roll yourself one of these?

DAVIES

(*turning*) What? No, no, I never smoke a cigarette.

Pause. He comes forward.

I'll tell you what, though. I'll have a bit of that tobacco there for my pipe, if you like.

ASTON

(*handing him the tin*) Yes. Go on. Take some out of that.

DAVIES

That's kind of you, mister. Just enough to fill my pipe, that's all.

He takes a pipe from his pocket and fills it.

I had a tin, only … only a while ago. But it was knocked off. It was knocked off on the Great West Road.

He holds out the tin.

Where shall I put it?

ASTON

I'll take it.

DAVIES

(*handing the tin*) When he come at me tonight I told
him. Didn't I? You heard me tell him, didn't you?

ASTON

I saw him have a go at you.

DAVIES

Go at me? You wouldn't grumble. The filthy skate, an
old man like me, I've had dinner with the best.

Pause.

ASTON

Yes, I saw him have a go at you.

DAVIES

All them toe-rags, mate, got the manners of pigs. I
might have been on the road a few years but you can
take it from me I'm clean. I keep myself up. That's why
I left my wife. Fortnight after I married her, no, not so
much as that, no more than a week, I took the lid off a
saucepan, you know what was in it? A pile of her
underclothing, unwashed. The pan for vegetables, it
was. The vegetable pan. That's when I left her and I
haven't seen her since.

DAVIES *turns, shambles across the room, comes face to
face with a statue of Buddha standing on the gas stove,
looks at it and turns.*

4

I've eaten my dinner off the best of plates. But I'm not young any more. I remember the days I was as handy as any of them. They didn't take any liberties with me. But I haven't been so well lately. I've had a few attacks.

Pause.

(*coming closer*) Did you see what happened with that one?

ASTON

I only got the end of it.

DAVIES

Comes up to me, parks a bucket of rubbish at me, tells me to take it out the back. It's not my job to take out the bucket! They got a boy there for taking out the bucket. I wasn't engaged to take out buckets. My job's cleaning the floor, clearing up the tables, doing a bit of washing-up, nothing to do with taking out buckets!

ASTON

Uh.

He crosses down right, to get the electric toaster.

DAVIES

(*following*) Yes, well say I had! Even if I had! Even if I was supposed to take out the bucket, who was this git to come up and give me orders? We got the same standing. He's not my boss. He's nothing superior to me.

ASTON

What was he, a Greek?

DAVIES

Not him, he was a Scotch. He was a Scotchman.

ASTON *goes back to his bed with the toaster and starts to unscrew the plug.* DAVIES *follows him.*

You got an eye of him, did you?

ASTON

Yes.

DAVIES

I told him what to do with his bucket. Didn't I? You heard. Look here, I said, I'm an old man, I said, where I was brought up we had some idea how to talk to old people with the proper respect, we was brought up with the right ideas, if I had a few years off me I'd ... I'd break you in half. That was after the guvnor give me the bullet. Making too much commotion, he says. Commotion, me! Look here, I said to him, I got my rights. I told him that. I might have been on the road but nobody's got more rights than I have. Let's have a bit of fair play, I said. Anyway, he give me the bullet.

He sits in the chair.

That's the sort of place.

Pause.

If you hadn't come out and stopped that Scotch git I'd be inside the hospital now. I'd have cracked my head on that pavement if he'd have landed. I'll get him. One night I'll get him. When I find myself around that direction.

ASTON *crosses to the plug box to get another plug.*

6

I wouldn't mind so much but I left all my belongings in that place, in the back room there. All of them, the lot there was, you see, in this bag. Every lousy blasted bit of all my bleeding belongings I left down there now. In the rush of it. I bet he's having a poke around in it now this very moment.

ASTON

I'll pop down sometime and pick them up for you.

ASTON *goes back to his bed and starts to fix the plug on the toaster.*

DAVIES

Anyway, I'm obliged to you, letting me ... letting me have a bit of a rest, like ... for a few minutes.

He looks about.

This your room?

ASTON

Yes.

DAVIES

You got a good bit of stuff here.

ASTON

Yes.

DAVIES

Must be worth a few bob, this ... put it all together.

Pause.

There's enough of it.

ASTON

There's a good bit of it, all right.

DAVIES

You sleep here, do you?

ASTON

Yes.

DAVIES

What, in that?

ASTON

Yes.

DAVIES

Yes, well, you'd be well out of the draught there.

ASTON

You don't get much wind.

DAVIES

You'd be well out of it. It's different when you're kipping out.

ASTON

Would be.

DAVIES

Nothing but wind then.

Pause.

ASTON

Yes, when the wind gets up it ...

Pause.

DAVIES

Yes ...

ASTON

Mmnn ...

Pause.

DAVIES

Gets very draughty.

ASTON

Ah.

DAVIES

I'm very sensitive to it.

ASTON

Are you?

DAVIES

Always have been.

Pause.

You got any more rooms then, have you?

ASTON

Where?

DAVIES

I mean, along the landing here ... up the landing there.

ASTON

They're out of commission.

DAVIES

Get away.

ASTON

They need a lot of doing to.

Slight pause.

DAVIES

What about downstairs?

ASTON

That's closed up. Needs seeing to ... The floors ...

Pause.

DAVIES

I was lucky you come into that caff. I might have been done by that Scotch git. I been left for dead more than once.

Pause.

I noticed that there was someone was living in the house next door.

ASTON

What?

DAVIES

(*gesturing*) I noticed ...

ASTON

Yes. There's people living all along the road.

DAVIES

Yes, I noticed the curtains pulled down there next door as we came along.

ASTON

They're neighbours.

Pause.

DAVIES

This your house then, is it?

Pause.

ASTON

I'm in charge.

DAVIES

You the landlord, are you?

He puts a pipe in his mouth and puffs without lighting it.

Yes. I noticed them heavy curtains pulled across next door as we came along. I noticed them heavy big curtains right across the window down there. I thought there must be someone living there.

ASTON

Family of Indians live there.

DAVIES

Blacks?

ASTON

I don't see much of them.

DAVIES

Blacks, eh?

DAVIES *stands and moves about.*

Well you've got some knick-knacks here all right, I'll say that. I don't like a bare room.

ASTON *joins* DAVIES *upstage centre.*

I'll tell you what, mate, you haven't got a spare pair of shoes?

11

Shoes?

ASTON *moves downstage right.*

DAVIES

Them bastards at the monastery let me down again.

ASTON

(*going to his bed*) Where?

DAVIES

Down in Luton. Monastery down at Luton . . . I got a
mate at Shepherd's Bush, you see . . .

ASTON

(*looking under his bed*) I might have a pair.

DAVIES

I got this mate at Shepherd's Bush. In the convenience.
Well, he was in the convenience. Run about the best
convenience they had.

He watches ASTON.

Run about the best one. Always slipped me a bit of
soap, any time I went in there. Very good soap. They
have to have the best soap. I was never without a piece
of soap, whenever I happened to be knocking about the
Shepherd's Bush area.

ASTON

(*emerging from under the bed with shoes*) Pair of brown.

DAVIES

He's gone now. Went. He was the one who put me on
to this monastery. Just the other side of Luton. He'd
heard they give away shoes.

ASTON

You've got to have a good pair of shoes.

DAVIES

Shoes? It's life and death to me. I had to go all the way
to Luton in these.

ASTON

What happened when you got there, then?

Pause.

DAVIES

I used to know a bootmaker in Acton. He was a good
mate to me.

Pause.

You know what that bastard monk said to me?

Pause.

How many more Blacks you got around here then?

ASTON

What?

DAVIES

You got any more Blacks around here?

ASTON

(*holding out the shoes*) See if these are any good.

DAVIES

You know what that bastard monk said to me?

He looks over to the shoes.

I think those'd be a bit small.

Would they?

No, don't look the right size.

Not bad trim.

Can't wear shoes that don't fit. Nothing worse. I said to this monk, here, I said, look here, mister, he opened the door, big door, he opened it, look here, mister, I said, I come all the way down here, look, I said, I showed him these, I said, you haven't got a pair of shoes, have you, a pair of shoes, I said, enough to keep me on my way. Look at these, they're nearly out, I said, they're no good to me. I heard you got a stock of shoes here. Piss off, he said to me. Now look here, I said, I'm an old man, you can't talk to me like that, I don't care who you are. If you don't piss off, he says, I'll kick you all the way to the gate. Now look here, I said, now wait a minute, all I'm asking for is a pair of shoes, you don't want to start taking liberties with me, it's taken me three days to get here, I said to him, three days without a bite, I'm worth a bite to eat, en I? Get out round the corner to the kitchen, he says, get out round the corner, and when you've had your meal, piss off out of it. I went round to this kitchen, see? Meal they give me! A bird, I tell you, a little bird, a little tiny bird, he could have ate it in under two minutes. Right, they said to me, you've had your meal, get off out of it. Meal? I said, what do you think I am, a dog? Nothing better than a dog. What do you think I am, a wild

animal? What about them shoes I come all the way
here to get I heard you was giving away? I've a good
mind to report you to your mother superior. One of
them, an Irish hooligan, come at me. I cleared out. I
took a short cut to Watford and picked up a pair there.
Got onto the North Circular, just past Hendon, the
sole come off, right where I was walking. Lucky I had
my old ones wrapped up, still carrying them, otherwise
I'd have been finished, man. So I've had to stay with
these, you see, they're gone, they're no good, all the
good's gone out of them.

ASTON

Try these.

DAVIES *takes the shoes, takes off his sandals and tries
them on.*

DAVIES

Not a bad pair of shoes.

He trudges round the room.

They're strong, all right. Yes. Not a bad shape of shoe.
This leather's hardy, en't? Very hardy. Some bloke tried
to flog me some suede the other day. I wouldn't wear
them. Can't beat leather, for wear. Suede goes off, it
creases, it stains for life in five minutes. You can't beat
leather. Yes. Good shoe this.

ASTON

Good.

DAVIES *waggles his feet.*

DAVIES

Don't fit though.

ASTON
Oh?

DAVIES
No. I got a very broad foot.

ASTON
Mmnn.

DAVIES
These are too pointed, you see.

ASTON
Ah.

DAVIES
They'd cripple me in a week. I mean these ones I got on, they're no good but at least they're comfortable. Not much cop, but I mean they don't hurt.

He takes them off and gives them back.

Thanks anyway, mister.

ASTON
I'll see what I can look out for you.

DAVIES
Good luck. I can't go on like this. Can't get from one place to another. And I'll have to be moving about, you see, try to get fixed up.

ASTON
Where you going to go?

DAVIES
Oh, I got one or two things in mind. I'm waiting for the weather to break.

Pause.

ASTON

(*attending to the toaster*) Would ... would you like to sleep here?

DAVIES

Here?

ASTON

You can sleep here if you like.

DAVIES

Here? Oh, I don't know about that.

Pause.

How long for?

ASTON

Till you ... get yourself fixed up.

DAVIES

(*sitting*) Ay well, that ...

ASTON

Get yourself sorted out...

DAVIES

Oh, I'll be fixed up ... pretty soon now...

Pause.

Where would I sleep?

ASTON

Here. The other rooms would ... would be no good to you.

DAVIES

(*rising, looking about*) Here? Where?

ASTON

(*rising, pointing upstage right*) There's a bed behind all that.

DAVIES

Oh, I see. Well, that's handy. Well, that's ... I tell you what, I might do that ... just till I get myself sorted out. You got enough furniture here.

ASTON

I picked it up. Just keeping it here for the time being. Thought it might come in handy.

DAVIES

This gas stove work, do it?

ASTON

No.

DAVIES

What do you do for a cup of tea?

ASTON

Nothing.

DAVIES

That's a bit rough.

DAVIES *observes the planks.*

You building something?

ASTON

I might build a shed out the back.

DAVIES

Carpenter, eh?

He turns to the lawn-mower.

Got a lawn?

ASTON

Have a look.

ASTON *lifts the sack at the window. They look out.*

DAVIES

Looks a bit thick.

ASTON

Overgrown.

DAVIES

What's that, a pond?

ASTON

Yes.

DAVIES

What you got, fish?

ASTON

No. There isn't anything in there.

Pause.

DAVIES

Where you going to put your shed?

ASTON

(*turning*) I'll have to clear the garden first.

DAVIES

You'd need a tractor, man.

ASTON

I'll get it done.

DAVIES

Carpentry, eh?

ASTON

(*standing still*) I like ... working with my hands.

DAVIES *picks up the statue of Buddha.*

DAVIES

What's this?

ASTON

(*taking and studying it*) That's a Buddha.

DAVIES

Get on.

ASTON

Yes. I quite like it. Picked it up in a ... in a shop.
Looked quite nice to me. Don't know why. What do
you think of these Buddhas?

DAVIES

Oh, they're ... they're all right, en't they?

ASTON

Yes, I was pleased when I got hold of this one. It's very
well made.

DAVIES *turns and peers under the sink.*

DAVIES

This the bed here, is it?

ASTON

(*moving to the bed*) We'll get rid of all that. The ladder'll fit under the bed.

They put the ladder under the bed.

DAVIES

(*indicating the sink*) What about this?

ASTON

I think that'll fit in under here as well.

DAVIES

I'll give you a hand.

They lift it.

It's a ton weight, en't?

ASTON

Under here.

DAVIES

This in use at all, then?

ASTON

No. I'll be getting rid of it. Here.

They place the sink under the bed.

There's a lavatory down the landing. It's got a sink in there. We can put this stuff over there.

They begin to move the coal bucket, shopping trolley, lawn-mower and sideboard drawers to the right wall.

DAVIES

(*stopping*) You don't share it, do you?

ASTON

What?

DAVIES

I mean you don't share the toilet with them Blacks, do you?

ASTON

They live next door.

DAVIES

They don't come in?

ASTON *puts a drawer against the wall.*

Because, you know ... I mean ... fair's fair ...

ASTON *goes to the bed, blows dust and shakes a blanket.*

ASTON

You see a blue case?

DAVIES

Blue case? Down here. Look. By the carpet.

ASTON *goes to the case, opens it, takes out a sheet and pillow and puts them on the bed.*

That's a nice sheet.

ASTON

The blanket'll be a bit dusty.

DAVIES

Don't you worry about that.

ASTON *stands upright, takes out his tobacco and begins to roll a cigarette. He goes to his bed and sits.*

ASTON

How are you off for money?

DAVIES

Oh well ... now, mister, if you want the truth ... I'm a
bit short.

ASTON *takes some coins from his pocket, sorts them,
and holds out five shillings.*

ASTON

Here's a few bob.

DAVIES

(*taking the coins*) Thank you, thank you, good luck. I
just happen to find myself a bit short. You see, I got
nothing for all that week's work I did last week. That's
the position, that's what it is.

Pause.

ASTON

I went into a pub the other day. Ordered a Guinness.
They gave it to me in a thick mug. I sat down but I
couldn't drink it. I can't drink Guinness from a thick
mug. I only like it out of a thin glass. I had a few sips
but I couldn't finish it.

ASTON *picks up a screwdriver and plug from the bed
and begins to poke the plug.*

DAVIES

(*with great feeling*) If only the weather would break!
Then I'd be able to get down to Sidcup!

ASTON

Sidcup?

23

DAVIES

The weather's so blasted bloody awful, how can I get down to Sidcup in these shoes?

ASTON

Why do you want to get down to Sidcup?

DAVIES

I got my papers there!

Pause.

ASTON

Your what?

DAVIES

I got my papers there!

Pause.

ASTON

What are they doing at Sidcup?

DAVIES

A man I know has got them. I left them with him. You see? They prove who I am! I can't move without them papers. They tell you who I am. You see! I'm stuck without them.

ASTON

Why's that?

DAVIES

You see, what it is, you see, I changed my name! Years ago. I been going around under an assumed name! That's not my real name.

ASTON

What name have you been going under?

DAVIES

Jenkins. Bernard Jenkins. That's my name. That's the name I'm known, anyway. But it's no good me going on with that name. I got no rights. I got an insurance card here.

He takes a card from his pocket.

Under the name of Jenkins. See? Bernard Jenkins. Look. It's got four stamps on it. Four of them. But I can't go along with these. That's not my real name, they'd find out, they'd have me in the nick. Four stamps. I haven't paid out pennies. I've paid out pounds. I've paid out pounds, not pennies. There's been other stamps, plenty, but they haven't put them on, the nigs, I never had enough time to go into it.

ASTON

They should have stamped your card.

DAVIES

It would have done no good! I'd have got nothing anyway. That's not my real name. If I take that card along I go in the nick.

ASTON

What's your real name, then?

DAVIES

Davies. Mac Davies. That was before I changed my name.

Pause.

It looks as though you want to sort all that out.

DAVIES

If only I could get down to Sidcup! I've been waiting for the weather to break. He's got my papers, this man I left them with, it's got it all down there, I could prove everything.

ASTON

How long's he had them?

DAVIES

What?

ASTON

How long's he had them?

DAVIES

Oh, must be ... it was in the war ... must be ... about near on fifteen year ago.

He suddenly becomes aware of the bucket and looks up.

ASTON

Any time you want to ... get into bed, just get in. Don't worry about me.

DAVIES

(*taking off his overcoat*) Eh, well, I think I will. I'm a bit ... a bit done in.

He steps out of his trousers, and holds them out.

Shall I put these on here?

ASTON

Yes.

DAVIES *puts the coat and trousers on the clothes horse.*

DAVIES
I see you got a bucket up here.

ASTON
Leak.

DAVIES *looks up.*

DAVIES
Well, I'll try your bed then. You getting in?

ASTON
I'm mending this plug.

DAVIES *looks at him and then at the gas stove.*

DAVIES
You ... you can't move this, eh?

ASTON
Bit heavy.

DAVIES
Yes.

DAVIES *gets into bed. He tests his weight and length.*

Not bad. Not bad. A fair bed. I think I'll sleep in this.

ASTON
I'll have to fix a proper shade on that bulb. The light's a
bit glaring.

DAVIES
Don't you worry about that, mister, don't you worry
about that.

He turns and puts the cover up.

ASTON *sits, poking his plug.*

The lights fade out. Darkness.

Lights up. Morning.

ASTON *is fastening his trousers, standing by the bed. He straightens his bed. He turns, goes to the centre of the room and looks at* DAVIES. *He turns, puts his jacket on, turns, goes towards* DAVIES *and looks down on him.*

He coughs. DAVIES *sits up abruptly.*

> DAVIES

What? What's this? What's this?

> ASTON

It's all right.

> DAVIES

(*staring*) What's this?

> ASTON

It's all right.

DAVIES *looks about.*

> DAVIES

Oh, yes.

ASTON *goes to his bed, picks up the plug and shakes it.*

> ASTON

Sleep well?

> DAVIES

Yes. Dead out. Must have been dead out.

ASTON *goes downstage right, collects the toaster and examines it.*

ASTON

You ... er ...

DAVIES

Eh?

ASTON

Were you dreaming or something?

DAVIES

Dreaming?

ASTON

Yes.

DAVIES

I don't dream. I've never dreamed.

ASTON

No, nor have I.

DAVIES

Nor me.

Pause.

Why you ask me that, then?

ASTON

You were making noises.

DAVIES

Who was?

ASTON

You were.

DAVIES *gets out of bed. He wears long underpants.*

DAVIES

Now, wait a minute. Wait a minute, what do you mean?
What kind of noises?

ASTON

You were making groans. You were jabbering.

DAVIES

Jabbering? Me?

ASTON

Yes.

DAVIES

I don't jabber, man. Nobody ever told me that before.

Pause.

What would I be jabbering about?

ASTON

I don't know.

DAVIES

I mean, where's the sense in it?

Pause.

Nobody ever told me that before.

Pause.

You got hold of the wrong bloke, mate.

ASTON

(*crossing to the bed with the toaster*) No. You woke me
up. I thought you might have been dreaming.

DAVIES

I wasn't dreaming. I never had a dream in my life.

30

Pause.

ASTON

Maybe it was the bed.

DAVIES

Nothing wrong with this bed.

ASTON

Might be a bit unfamiliar.

DAVIES

There's nothing unfamiliar about me with beds. I slept
in beds. I don't make noises just because I sleep in a
bed. I slept in plenty of beds.

Pause.

I tell you what, maybe it were them Blacks.

ASTON

What?

DAVIES

Them noises.

ASTON

What Blacks?

DAVIES

Them you got. Next door. Maybe it were them Blacks
making noises, coming up through the walls.

ASTON

Hmmnn.

DAVIES

That's my opinion.

ASTON *puts down the plug and moves to the door.*

Where you going, you going out?

ASTON

Yes.

DAVIES

(*seizing the sandals*) Wait a minute then, just a minute.

ASTON

What you doing?

DAVIES

(*putting on the sandals*) I better come with you.

ASTON

Why?

DAVIES

I mean, I better come out with you, anyway.

ASTON

Why?

DAVIES

Well ... don't you want me to go out?

ASTON

What for?

DAVIES

I mean ... when you're out. Don't you want me to get out ... when you're out?

ASTON

You don't have to go out.

DAVIES

You mean . . . I can stay here?

ASTON

Do what you like. You don't have to come out just because I go out.

DAVIES

You don't mind me staying here?

ASTON

I've got a couple of keys.

He goes to a box by his bed and finds them.

This door and the front door.

He hands them to DAVIES.

DAVIES

Thanks very much, the best of luck.

Pause. ASTON *stands.*

ASTON

I think I'll take a stroll down the road. A little . . . kind of a shop. Man there'd got a jig saw the other day. I quite liked the look of it.

DAVIES

A jig saw, mate?

ASTON

Yes. Could be very useful.

DAVIES

Yes.

Slight pause.

What's that then, exactly, then?

ASTON *walks up to the window and looks out.*

ASTON

A jig saw? Well, it comes from the same family as the fret saw. But it's an appliance, you see. You have to fix it on to a portable drill.

DAVIES

Ah, that's right. They're very handy.

ASTON

They are, yes.

Pause.

You know, I was sitting in a café the other day. I happened to be sitting at the same table as this woman. Well, we started to ... we started to pick up a bit of a conversation. I don't know ... about her holiday, it was, where she'd been. She'd been down to the south coast. I can't remember where though. Anyway, we were just sitting there, having this bit of a conversation ... then suddenly she put her hand over to mine ... and she said, how would you like me to have a look at your body?

DAVIES

Get out of it.

Pause.

ASTON

Yes. To come out with it just like that, in the middle of this conversation. Struck me as a bit odd.

DAVIES

They've said the same thing to me.

ASTON

Have they?

DAVIES

Women? There's many a time they've come up to me and asked me more or less the same question.

Pause.

ASTON

What did you say your name was?

DAVIES

Bernard Jenkins is my assumed one.

ASTON

No, your other one?

DAVIES

Davies. Mac Davies.

ASTON

Welsh, are you?

DAVIES

Eh?

ASTON

You Welsh?

Pause.

DAVIES

Well, I been around, you know ... what I mean ... I been about ...

ASTON

Where were you born then?

DAVIES

(*darkly*) What do you mean?

ASTON

Where were you born?

DAVIES

I was ... uh ... oh, it's a bit hard, like, to set your mind
back ... see what I mean ... going back ... a good way
... lose a bit of track, like ... you know ...

ASTON

(*going to below the fireplace*) See this plug? Switch it on
here, if you like. This little fire.

DAVIES

Right, mister.

ASTON

Just plug in here.

DAVIES

Right, mister.

ASTON *goes towards the door.*

(*anxiously*) What do I do?

ASTON

Just switch it on, that's all. The fire'll come on.

DAVIES

I tell you what. I won't bother about it.

ASTON

No trouble.

36

DAVIES

No, I don't go in for them things much.

ASTON

Should work. (*Turning*) Right.

DAVIES

Eh, I was going to ask you, mister, what about this stove? I mean, do you think it's going to be letting out any ... what do you think?

ASTON

It's not connected.

DAVIES

You see, the trouble is, it's right on top of my bed, you see? What I got to watch is nudging ... one of them gas taps with my elbow when I get up, you get my meaning?

He goes round to the other side of stove and examines it.

ASTON

There's nothing to worry about.

DAVIES

Now look here, don't you worry about it. All I'll do, I'll keep an eye on these taps every now and again, like, you see. See they're switched off. You leave it to me.

ASTON

I don't think ...

DAVIES

(*coming round*) Eh, mister, just one thing ... eh ... you couldn't slip me a couple of bob, for a cup of tea, just, you know?

ASTON

I gave you a few bob last night.

DAVIES

Eh, so you did. So you did. I forgot. Went clean out of
my mind. That's right. Thank you, mister. Listen.
You're sure now, you're sure you don't mind me staying
here? I mean, I'm not the sort of man who wants to
take any liberties.

ASTON

No, that's all right.

DAVIES

I might get down to Wembley later on in the day.

ASTON

Uh-uh.

DAVIES

There's a caff down there, you see, might be able to get
fixed up there. I was there, see? I know they were a bit
short-handed. They might be in the need of a bit of
staff.

ASTON

When was that?

DAVIES

Eh? Oh, well, that was ... near on ... that'll be ...
that'll be a little while ago now. But of course what it is,
they can't find the right kind of people in these places.
What they want to do, they're trying to do away with
these foreigners, you see, in catering. They want an
Englishman to pour their tea, that's what they want,
that's what they're crying out for. It's only common

sense, en't? Oh, I got all that under way ... that's ... uh ... that's ... what I'll be doing.

Pause.

If only I could get down there.

ASTON

Mmnn.

ASTON *moves to the door.*

Well, I'll be seeing you then.

DAVIES

Yes. Right.

ASTON *goes out and closes the door.*

DAVIES *stands still. He waits a few seconds, then goes to the door, opens it, looks out, closes it, stands with his back to it, turns swiftly, opens it, looks out, comes back, closes the door, finds the keys in his pocket, tries one, tries the other, locks the door. He looks about the room. He then goes quickly to* ASTON*'s bed, bends, brings out the pair of shoes and examines them.*

Not a bad pair of shoes. Bit pointed.

He puts them back under the bed. He examines the area by ASTON*'s bed, picks up a vase and looks into it, then picks up a box and shakes it.*

Screws!

He sees paint buckets at the top of the bed, goes to them, and examines them.

Paint. What's he going to paint?

He puts the bucket down, comes to the centre of the room, looks up at bucket, and grimaces.

I'll have to find out about that.

He crosses right, and picks up a blow-lamp.

He's got some stuff in here.

He picks up the Buddha and looks at it.

Full of stuff. Look at all this.

His eye falls on the piles of papers.

What's he got all those papers for? Damn pile of papers.

He goes to a pile and touches it. The pile wobbles. He steadies it.

Hold it, hold it!

He holds the pile and pushes the papers back into place.

The door opens.

MICK *comes in, puts the key in his pocket, and closes the door silently. He stands at the door and watches* DAVIES.

What's he got all these papers for?

DAVIES *climbs over the rolled carpet to the blue case.*

Had a sheet and pillow ready in here.

He opens the case.

Nothing.

He shuts the case.

Still, I had a sleep though. I don't make no noises.

He looks at the window.

What's this?

He picks up another case and tries to open it. MICK *moves upstage, silently.*

Locked.

He puts it down and moves downstage.

Must be something in it.

He picks up a sideboard drawer, rummages in the contents, then puts it down.

MICK *slides across the room.*

DAVIES *half turns,* MICK *seizes his arm and forces it up his back.* DAVIES *screams.*

Uuuuuuuhhh! Uuuuuuuhhh! What! What! What! Uuuuuuuhhh!

MICK *swiftly forces him to the floor, with* DAVIES *struggling, grimacing, whimpering and staring.*

MICK *holds his arm, puts his other hand to his lips, then puts his hand to* DAVIES' *lips.* DAVIES *quietens.* MICK *lets him go.* DAVIES *writhes.* MICK *holds out a warning finger. He then squats down to regard* DAVIES. *He regards him, then stands looking down on him.* DAVIES *massages his arm, watching* MICK. MICK *turns slowly to look at the room. He goes to* DAVIES' *bed and uncovers it. He turns, goes to the clothes horse and picks up* DAVIES' *trousers.* DAVIES *starts to rise.* MICK *presses him down with his foot and stands over him.*

Finally he removes his foot. He examines the trousers and throws them back. DAVIES *remains on the floor, crouched.* MICK *slowly goes to the chair, sits, and watches* DAVIES, *expressionless.*

Silence.

MICK

What's the game?

Curtain.

Act Two

A few seconds later.

MICK *is seated,* DAVIES *on the floor, half seated, crouched.*

Silence.

MICK
Well?

DAVIES
Nothing, nothing. Nothing.

A drip sounds in the bucket overhead. They look up.
MICK *looks back to* DAVIES.

MICK
What's your name?

DAVIES
I don't know you. I don't know who you are.

Pause.

MICK
Eh?

DAVIES
Jenkins.

MICK
Jenkins?

43

                              DAVIES
Yes.

                               MICK
Jen ... kins.

Pause.

You sleep here last night?

                              DAVIES
Yes.

                               MICK
Sleep well?

                              DAVIES
Yes.

                               MICK
I'm awfully glad. It's awfully nice to meet you.

Pause.

What did you say your name was?

                              DAVIES
Jenkins.

                               MICK
I beg your pardon?

                              DAVIES
Jenkins!

Pause.

                               MICK
Jen ... kins.

A drip sounds in the bucket. DAVIES *looks up.*

You remind me of my uncle's brother. He was always on the move, that man. Never without his passport. Had an eye for the girls. Very much your build. Bit of an athlete. Long-jump specialist. He had a habit of demonstrating different run-ups in the drawing-room round about Christmas time. Had a penchant for nuts. That's what it was. Nothing else but a penchant. Couldn't eat enough of them. Peanuts, walnuts, brazil nuts, monkey nuts, wouldn't touch a piece of fruit cake. Had a marvellous stop-watch. Picked it up in Hong Kong. The day after they chucked him out of the Salvation Army. Used to go in number four for Beckenham Reserves. That was before he got his Gold Medal. Had a funny habit of carrying his fiddle on his back. Like a papoose. I think there was a bit of the Red Indian in him. To be honest, I've never made out how he came to be my uncle's brother. I've often thought that maybe it was the other way round. I mean that my uncle was his brother and he was my uncle. But I never called him uncle. As a matter of fact I called him Sid. My mother called him Sid too. It was a funny business. Your spitting image he was. Married a Chinaman and went to Jamaica.

Pause.

I hope you slept well last night.

DAVIES
Listen! I don't know who you are!

MICK
What bed you sleep in?

45

DAVIES

Now look here –

MICK

Eh?

DAVIES

That one.

MICK

Not the other one?

DAVIES

No.

MICK

Choosy.

Pause.

How do you like my room?

DAVIES

Your room?

MICK

Yes.

DAVIES

This ain't your room. I don't know who you are. I ain't
never seen you before.

MICK

You know, believe it or not, you've got a funny kind of
resemblance to a bloke I once knew in Shoreditch.
Actually he lived in Aldgate. I was staying with a cousin
in Camden Town. This chap, he used to have a pitch in
Finsbury Park, just by the bus depot. When I got to

46

know him I found out he was brought up in Putney.
That didn't make any difference to me. I know quite a
few people who were born in Putney. Even if they
weren't born in Putney they were born in Fulham. The
only trouble was, he wasn't born in Putney, he was only
brought up in Putney. It turned out he was born in the
Caledonian Road, just before you get to the Nag's
Head. His old mum was still living at the Angel. All the
buses passed right by the door. She could get a 38, 581,
30 or 38A, take her down the Essex Road to Dalston
Junction in next to no time. Well, of course, if she got
the 30 he'd take her up Upper Street way, round by
Highbury Corner and down to St Paul's Church, but
she'd get to Dalston Junction just the same in the end. I
used to leave my bike in her garden on my way to
work. Yes, it was a curious affair. Dead spit of you he
was. Bit bigger round the nose but there was nothing
in it.

Pause.

Did you sleep here last night?

DAVIES

Yes.

MICK

Sleep well?

DAVIES

Yes!

MICK

Did you have to get up in the night?

DAVIES

No!

Pause.

MICK

What's your name?

DAVIES

(*shifting, about to rise*) Now look here!

MICK

What?

DAVIES

Jenkins!

MICK

Jen ... kins.

DAVIES *makes a sudden move to rise. A violent bellow from* MICK *sends him back.*

A shout.

Sleep here last night?

DAVIES

Yes ...

MICK

(*continuing at great pace*) How'd you sleep?

DAVIES

I slept –

MICK

Sleep well?

DAVIES

Now look –

MICK

What bed?

DAVIES

That –

MICK

Not the other?

DAVIES

No!

MICK

Choosy.

Pause.

(quietly) Choosy.

Pause.

(again amiable) What sort of sleep did you have in that bed?

DAVIES

(banging on floor) All right!

MICK

You weren't uncomfortable?

DAVIES

(groaning) All right!

MICK *stands, and moves to him.*

MICK

You a foreigner?

49

DAVIES

No.

MICK

Born and bred in the British Isles?

DAVIES

I was!

MICK

What did they teach you?

Pause.

How did you like my bed?

Pause.

That's my bed. You want to mind you don't catch a draught.

DAVIES

From the bed?

MICK

No, now, up your arse.

DAVIES *stares warily at* MICK, *who turns.* DAVIES *scrambles to the clothes horse and seizes his trousers.* MICK *turns swiftly and grabs them.* DAVIES *lunges for them.* MICK *holds out a hand warningly.*

You intending to settle down here?

DAVIES

Give me my trousers then.

MICK

You settling down for a long stay?

DAVIES

Give me my bloody trousers!

MICK

Why, where you going?

DAVIES

Give me and I'm going, I'm going to Sidcup!

MICK *flicks the trousers in* DAVIES' *face several times.*

DAVIES *retreats.*

Pause.

MICK

You know, you remind me of a bloke I bumped into
once, just the other side of the Guildford by-pass –

DAVIES

I was brought here!

Pause.

MICK

Pardon?

DAVIES

I was brought here! I was brought here!

MICK

Brought here? Who brought you here?

DAVIES

Man who lives here ... he ...

Pause.

MICK

Fibber.

DAVIES

I was brought here, last night ... met him in a caff ... I was working ... I got the bullet ... I was working there ... bloke saved me from a punch up, brought me here, brought me right here.

Pause.

MICK

I'm afraid you're a born fibber, en't you? You're speaking to the owner. This is my room. You're standing in my house.

DAVIES

It's his ... he seen me all right ... he....

MICK

(*pointing to* DAVIES' *bed*) That's my bed.

DAVIES

What about that, then?

MICK

That's my mother's bed.

DAVIES

Well she wasn't in it last night!

MICK

(*moving to him*) Now don't get perky, son, don't get perky. Keep your hands off my old mum.

DAVIES

I ain't ... I haven't....

MICK

Don't get out of your depth, friend, don't start taking liberties with my old mother, let's have a bit of respect.

DAVIES

I got respect, you won't find anyone with more respect.

MICK

Well, stop telling me all these fibs.

DAVIES

Now listen to me, I never seen you before, have I?

MICK

Never seen my mother before either, I suppose?

Pause.

I think I'm coming to the conclusion that you're an old rogue. You're nothing but an old scoundrel.

DAVIES

Now wait –

MICK

Listen, son. Listen, sonny. You stink.

DAVIES

You ain't got no right to –

MICK

You're stinking the place out. You're an old robber, there's no getting away from it. You're an old skate. You don't belong in a nice place like this. You're an old barbarian. Honest. You got no business wandering about in an unfurnished flat. I could charge seven quid a week for this if I wanted to. Get a taker tomorrow. Three hundred and fifty a year exclusive. No argument. I mean, if that sort of money's in your range don't be afraid to say so. Here you are. Furniture and fittings, I'll take four hundred or the nearest offer. Rateable value ninety quid for the annum. You can reckon water, heating and lighting at close on fifty. That'll cost you eight hundred and ninety if you're all that keen. Say the word and I'll have my solicitors draft you out a contract. Otherwise I've got the van outside, I can run you to the police station in five minutes, have you in for trespassing, loitering with intent, daylight robbery, filching, thieving and stinking the place out. What do you say? Unless you're really keen on a straightforward purchase. Of course, I'll get my brother to decorate it up for you first. I've got a brother who's a number one decorator. He'll decorate it up for you. If you want more space, there's four more rooms along the landing ready to go. Bathroom, living-room, bedroom and nursery. You can have this as your study. This brother I mentioned, he's just about to start on the other rooms. Yes, just about to start. So what do you say? Eight hundred odd for this room or three thousand down for the whole upper storey. On the other hand, if you prefer to approach it in the long-term way I know an insurance firm in West Ham'll be pleased to handle the deal for you. No strings attached, open and above board, untarnished record; twenty per cent interest, fifty per cent deposit; down payments, back payments, family allowances, bonus schemes, remission of term for good behaviour, six months lease, yearly examination of the relevant archives, tea laid on, disposal of shares, benefit extension, compensation on cessation, comprehensive indemnity against Riot, Civil Commotion, Labour Disturbances, Storm, Tempest, Thunderbolt, Larceny or Cattle all subject to a daily check and double check. Of course we'd need a signed declaration from your personal medical attendant as assurance that you possess the requisite fitness to carry the can, won't we? Who do you bank with?

Pause.

Who do you bank with?

The door opens. ASTON *comes in.* MICK *turns and drops the trousers.* DAVIES *picks them up and puts them on.* ASTON, *after a glance at the other two, goes to his bed, places a bag which he is carrying on it, sits down and resumes fixing the toaster.* DAVIES *retreats to his corner.* MICK *sits in the chair.*

Silence.

A drip sounds in the bucket. They all look up.

Silence.

You still got that leak.

ASTON

Yes.

Pause.

It's coming from the roof.

MICK

From the roof, eh?

ASTON

Yes.

Pause.

I'll have to tar it over.

                    MICK

You're going to tar it over?

                    ASTON

Yes.

                    MICK

What?

                    ASTON

The cracks.

Pause.

                    MICK

You'll be tarring over the cracks on the roof.

                    ASTON

Yes.

Pause.

                    MICK

Think that'll do it?

                    ASTON

It'll do it, for the time being.

                    MICK

Uh.   ─────────

Pause.

                    DAVIES

(*abruptly*) What do you do – ?

They both look at him.

What do you do ... when that bucket's full?

                    56

Pause.

ASTON

Empty it.

Pause.

MICK

I was telling my friend you were about to start
decorating the other rooms.

ASTON

Yes.

Pause.

(*to* DAVIES) I got your bag.

DAVIES

Oh.

Crossing to him and taking it.

Oh thanks, mister, thanks. Give it to you, did they?

DAVIES *crosses back with the bag.*

MICK *rises and snatches it.*

MICK

What's this?

DAVIES

Give us it, that's my bag!

MICK

(*warding him off*) I've seen this bag before.

DAVIES

That's my bag!

57

MICK

(*eluding him*) This bag's very familiar.

DAVIES

What do you mean?

MICK

Where'd you get it?

ASTON

(*rising, to them*) Scrub it.

DAVIES

That's mine.

MICK

Whose?

DAVIES

It's mine! Tell him it's mine!

MICK

This your bag?

DAVIES

Give me it!

ASTON

Give it to him.

MICK

What? Give him what?

DAVIES

That bloody bag!

MICK

(*slipping it behind the gas stove*) What bag?

(*to* DAVIES) What bag?

DAVIES

(*moving*) Look here!

MICK

(*facing him*) Where you going?

DAVIES

I'm going to get ... my old ...

MICK

Watch your step, sonny! You're knocking at the door
when no one's at home. Don't push it too hard. You
come busting into a private house, laying your hands on
anything you can lay your hands on. Don't overstep the
mark, son.

ASTON *picks up the bag.*

DAVIES

You thieving bastard ... you thieving skate ... let me
get my –

ASTON

Here you are.

ASTON *offers the bag to* DAVIES.

MICK *grabs it.* ASTON *takes it.*

MICK *grabs it.* DAVIES *reaches for it.*

ASTON *takes it.* MICK *reaches for it.*

ASTON *gives it to* DAVIES. MICK *grabs it.*

Pause.

ASTON *takes it.* DAVIES *takes it.* MICK *takes it.* DAVIES
reaches for it. ASTON *takes it.*

Pause.

ASTON *gives it to* MICK. MICK *gives it to* DAVIES.

DAVIES *grasps it to him.*

Pause.

MICK *looks at* ASTON. DAVIES *moves away with the bag.*

He drops it.

Pause.

They watch him. He picks it up. Goes to his bed, and sits.

ASTON *goes to his bed, sits, and begins to roll a cigarette.*

MICK *stands still.*

Pause.

A drip sounds in the bucket. They all look up.

Pause.

How did you get on at Wembley?

DAVIES
Well, I didn't get down there.

Pause.

No. I couldn't make it.

MICK *goes to the door and exits.*

ASTON
I had a bit of bad luck with that jig saw. When I got there it had gone.

Pause.

DAVIES

Who was that feller?

ASTON

He's my brother.

DAVIES

Is he? He's a bit of a joker, en' he?

ASTON

Uh.

DAVIES

Yes ... he's a real joker.

ASTON

He's got a sense of humour.

DAVIES

Yes, I noticed.

Pause.

He's a real joker, that lad, you can see that.

Pause.

ASTON

Yes, he tends ... he tends to see the funny side of things.

DAVIES

Well, he's got a sense of humour, en' he?

ASTON

Yes.

DAVIES

Yes, you could tell that.

Pause.

I could tell the first time I saw him he had his own way of looking at things.

ASTON *stands, goes to the sideboard drawer, right, picks up the statue of Buddha, and puts it on the gas stove.*

ASTON

I'm supposed to be doing up the upper part of the house for him.

DAVIES

What ... you mean ... you mean it's his house?

ASTON

Yes. I'm supposed to be decorating this landing for him. Make a flat out of it.

DAVIES

What does he do, then?

ASTON

He's in the building trade. He's got his own van.

DAVIES

He don't live here, do he?

ASTON

Once I get that shed up outside ... I'll be able to give a bit more thought to the flat, you see. Perhaps I can knock up one or two things for it.

He walks to the window.

I can work with my hands, you see. That's one thing I can do. I never knew I could. But I can do all sorts of

things now, with my hands. You know, manual things.
When I get that shed up out there ... I'll have a
workshop, you see. I ... could do a bit of woodwork.
Simple woodwork, to start. Working with ... good
wood.

Pause.

Of course, there's a lot to be done to this place. What I
think, though, I think I'll put in a partition ... in one of
the rooms along the landing. I think it'll take it. You know
... they've got these screens ... you know ... Oriental.
They break up a room with them. Make it into two parts.
I could either do that or I could have a partition. I could
knock them up, you see, if I had a workshop.

Pause.

Anyway, I think I've decided on the partition.

Pause.

DAVIES

Eh, look here, I been thinking. This ain't my bag.

ASTON

Oh. No.

DAVIES

No, this ain't my bag. My bag, it was another kind of
bag altogether, you see. I know what they've done.
What they done, they kept my bag, and they given you
another one altogether.

ASTON

No ... what happened was, someone had gone off with
your bag.

63

DAVIES

(*rising*) That's what I said!

ASTON

Anyway, I picked that bag up somewhere else. It's got a few ... pieces of clothes in it too. He let me have the whole lot cheap.

DAVIES

(*opening the bag*) Any shoes?

DAVIES *takes two check shirts, bright red and bright green, from the bag. He holds them up.*

Check.

ASTON

Yes.

DAVIES

Yes ... well, I know about these sort of shirts, you see. Shirts like these, they don't go far in the winter-time. I mean, that's one thing I know for a fact. No, what I need, is a kind of a shirt with stripes, a good solid shirt, with stripes going down. That's what I want.

He takes from the bag a deep-red velvet smoking-jacket.

What's this?

ASTON

It's a smoking-jacket.

DAVIES

A smoking-jacket?

He feels it.

This ain't a bad piece of cloth. I'll see how it fits.

He tries it on.

You ain't got a mirror here, have you?

ASTON

I don't think I have.

DAVIES

Well, it don't fit too bad. How do you think it looks?

ASTON

Looks all right.

DAVIES

Well, I won't say no to this, then.

ASTON *picks up the plug and examines it.*

No, I wouldn't say no to this.

Pause.

ASTON

You could be ... caretaker here, if you liked.

DAVIES

What?

ASTON

You could ... look after the place, if you liked ... you know, the stairs and the landing, the front steps, keep an eye on it. Polish the bells.

DAVIES

Bells?

ASTON

I'll be fixing a few, down by the front door. Brass.

DAVIES

Caretaking, eh?

ASTON

Yes.

DAVIES

Well, I ... I never done caretaking before, you know ...
I mean to say ... I never ... what I mean to say is ... I
never been a caretaker before.

Pause.

ASTON

How do you feel about being one, then?

DAVIES

Well, I reckon ... Well, I'd have to know ... you
know....

ASTON

What sort of ...

DAVIES

Yes, what sort of ... you know ...

Pause.

ASTON

Well, I mean ...

DAVIES

I mean, I'd have to ... I'd have to ...

ASTON

Well, I could tell you ...

DAVIES

That's ... that's it ... you see ... you get my meaning?

66

ASTON

When the time comes ...

DAVIES

I mean, that's what I'm getting at, you see ...

ASTON

More or less exactly what you ...

DAVIES

You see, what I mean to say ... what I'm getting at is ...
I mean, what sort of jobs ...

Pause.

ASTON

Well, there's things like the stairs ... and the ... the
bells ...

DAVIES

But it'd be a matter ... wouldn't it ... it'd be a matter of
a broom ... isn't it?

ASTON

Yes, and of course, you'd need a few brushes.

DAVIES

You'd need implements ... you see ... you'd need a
good few implements ...

ASTON *takes a white overall from a nail over his bed,
and shows it to* DAVIES.

ASTON

You could wear this, if you liked.

DAVIES

Well ... that's nice, en't?

ASTON

It'd keep the dust off.

DAVIES

(*putting it on*) Yes, this'd keep the dust off, all right.
Well off. Thanks very much, mister.

ASTON

You see, what we could do, we could ... I could fit a
bell at the bottom, outside the front door, with
"Caretaker" on it. And you could answer any queries.

DAVIES

Oh, I don't know about that.

ASTON

Why not?

DAVIES

Well, I mean, you don't know who might come up them
front steps, do you? I got to be a bit careful.

ASTON

Why, someone after you?

DAVIES

After me? Well, I could have that Scotch git coming
looking after me, couldn't I? All I'd do, I'd hear the bell,
I'd go down there, open the door, who might be there,
any Harry might be there. I could be buggered as easy
as that, man. They might be there after my card, I mean
look at it, here I am, I only got four stamps, on this
card, here it is, look, four stamps, that's all I got, I ain't
got any more, that's all I got, they ring the bell called
Caretaker, they'd have me in, that's what they'd do, I
wouldn't stand a chance. Of course I got plenty of other

cards lying about, but they don't know that, and I can't tell them, can I, because then they'd find out I was going about under an assumed name. You see, the name I call myself now, that's not my real name. My real name's not the one I'm using, you see. It's different. You see, the name I go under now ain't my real one. It's assumed.

Silence.

The lights fade to blackout.

Then up to dim light through the window.

A door bangs.

Sound of a key in the door of the room.

DAVIES *enters, closes the door, and tries the light switch, on, off, on, off.*

DAVIES
(*muttering*) What's this?

He switches on and off.

What's the matter with this damn light?

He switches on and off.

Aaah. Don't tell me the damn light's gone now.

Pause.

What'll I do? Damn light's gone now. Can't see a thing.

Pause.

What'll I do now?

He moves, stumbles.

69

Ah God, what's that? Give me a light. Wait a minute.

He feels for matches in his pocket, takes out a box and lights one. The match goes out. The box falls.

Aah! Where is it?

Stooping.

Where's the bloody box?

The box is kicked.

What's that? What? Who's that? What's that?

Pause. He moves.

Where's my box? It was down here. Who's this? Who's moving it?

Silence.

Come on. Who's this? Who's this got my box?

Pause.

Who's in here?

Pause.

I got a knife here. I'm ready. Come on then, who are you?

He moves, stumbles, falls and cries out.

Silence.

A faint whimper from DAVIES. *He gets up.*

All right!

He stands. Heavy breathing.

70

Suddenly the electrolux starts to hum. A figure moves with it, guiding it. The nozzle moves along the floor after DAVIES, *who skips, dives away from it and falls, breathlessly.*

Ah, ah, ah, ah, ah, ah! Get away-y-y-y-y!

The electrolux stops. The figure jumps on ASTON'S *bed.*

I'm ready for you! I'm … I'm … I'm here!

The figure takes out the electrolux plug from the light socket and fits the bulb. The light goes on. DAVIES *flattens himself against right wall, knife in hand.* MICK *stands on the bed, holding the plug.*

MICK
I was just doing some spring cleaning.

He gets down.

There used to be a wall plug for this electrolux. But it doesn't work. I had to fit it in the light socket.

He puts the electrolux plug under ASTON'S *bed.*

How do you think the place is looking? I gave it a good going over.

Pause.

We take it in turns, once a fortnight, my brother and me, to give the place a thorough going over. I was working late tonight, I only just got here. But I thought I better get on with it, as it's my turn.

Pause.

It's not that I actually live here. I don't. As a matter of

fact I live somewhere else. But after all, I'm responsible for the upkeep of the premises, en' I? Can't help being house-proud.

He moves towards DAVIES *and indicates the knife.*

What are you waving that about for?

DAVIES

You come near me ...

MICK

I'm sorry if I gave you a start. But I had you in mind too, you know. I mean, my brother's guest. We got to think of your comfort, en't we? Don't want the dust to get up your nose. How long you thinking of staying here, by the way? As a matter of fact, I was going to suggest that we'd lower your rent, make it just a nominal sum, I mean until you get fixed up. Just nominal, that's all.

Pause.

Still, if you're going to be spiky, I'll have to reconsider the whole proposition.

Pause.

Eh, you're not thinking of doing any violence on me, are you? You're not the violent sort, are you?

DAVIES

(*vehemently*) I keep myself to myself, mate. But if anyone starts with me though, they know what they got coming.

MICK

I can believe that.

DAVIES

You do. I been all over, see? You understand my
meaning? I don't mind a bit of a joke now and then, but
anyone'll tell you ... that no one starts anything with
me.

MICK

I get what you mean, yes.

DAVIES

I can be pushed so far ... but ...

MICK

No further.

DAVIES

That's it.

MICK *sits on junk down right.*

What you doing?

MICK

No, I just want to say that ... I'm very impressed by
that.

DAVIES

Eh?

MICK

I'm very impressed by what you've just said.

Pause.

Yes, that's impressive, that is.

Pause.

I'm impressed, anyway.

DAVIES

You know what I'm talking about then?

MICK

Yes, I know. I think we understand one another.

DAVIES

Uh? Well ... I'll tell you ... I'd ... I'd like to think that.
You been playing me about, you know. I don't know
why. I never done you no harm.

MICK

No, you know what it was? We just got off on the
wrong foot. That's all it was.

ASTON

Ay, we did.

DAVIES *joins* MICK *in junk*.

MICK

Like a sandwich?

DAVIES

What?

MICK

(*taking a sandwich from his pocket*) Have one of these.

DAVIES

Don't you pull anything.

MICK

No, you're still not understanding me. I can't help being
interested in any friend of my brother's. I mean, you're
my brother's friend, aren't you?

DAVIES

Well, I . . . I wouldn't put it as far as that.

MICK

Don't you find him friendly, then?

DAVIES

Well, I wouldn't say we was all that friends. I mean, he
done me no harm, but I wouldn't say he was any
particular friend of mine. What's in that sandwich,
then?

MICK

Cheese.

DAVIES

That'll do me.

MICK

Take one.

DAVIES

Thank you, mister.

MICK

I'm sorry to hear my brother's not very friendly.

DAVIES

He's friendly, he's friendly, I didn't say he wasn't . . .

MICK

(taking a salt-cellar from his pocket) Salt?

DAVIES

No thanks.

He munches the sandwich.

I just can't exactly . . . make him out.

75

MICK

(*feeling in his pocket*) I forgot the pepper.

DAVIES

Just can't get the hang of him, that's all.

MICK

I had a bit of beetroot somewhere. Must have mislaid it.

Pause.

DAVIES *chews the sandwich.* MICK *watches him eat. He then rises and strolls downstage.*

Uuh ... listen ... can I ask your advice? I mean, you're a man of the world. Can I ask your advice about something?

DAVIES

You go right ahead.

MICK

Well, what it is, you see, I'm ... I'm a bit worried about my brother.

DAVIES

Your brother?

MICK

Yes ... you see, his trouble is ...

DAVIES

What?

MICK

Well, it's not a very nice thing to say...

DAVIES

(*rising, coming downstage*) Go on now, you say it.

MICK *looks at him.*

MICK

He doesn't like work.

Pause.

DAVIES

Go on!

MICK

No, he just doesn't like work, that's his trouble.

DAVIES

Is that a fact?

MICK

It's a terrible thing to have to say about your own
brother.

DAVIES

Ay.

MICK

He's just shy of it. Very shy of it.

DAVIES

I know that sort.

MICK

You know the type?

DAVIES

I've met them.

MICK

I mean, I want to get him going in the world.

DAVIES

Stands to reason, man.

MICK

If you got an older brother you want to push him on, you want to see him make his way. Can't have him idle, he's only doing himself harm. That's what I say.

DAVIES

Yes.

MICK

But he won't buckle down to the job.

DAVIES

He don't like work.

MICK

Work shy.

DAVIES

Sounds like it to me.

MICK

You've met the type, have you?

DAVIES

Me? I know that sort.

MICK

Yes.

DAVIES

I know that sort. I've met them.

MICK

Causing me great anxiety. You see, I'm a working man: I'm a tradesman. I've got my own van.

DAVIES

Is that a fact?

MICK

He's supposed to be doing a little job for me ... I keep
him here to do a little job ... but I don't know ... I'm
coming to the conclusion he's a slow worker.

Pause.

What would your advice be?

DAVIES

Well ... he's a funny bloke, your brother.

MICK

What?

DAVIES

I was saying, he's ... he's a bit of a funny bloke, your
brother.

MICK *stares at him.*

MICK

Funny? Why?

DAVIES

Well ... he's funny ...

MICK

What's funny about him?

Pause.

DAVIES

Not liking work.

MICK

What's funny about that?

DAVIES

Nothing.

Pause.

MICK

I don't call it funny.

DAVIES

Nor me.

MICK

You don't want to start getting hypercritical.

DAVIES

No, no, I wasn't that, I wasn't ... I was only saying ...

MICK

Don't get too glib.

DAVIES

Look, all I meant was –

MICK

Cut it!

Briskly.

Look! I got a proposition to make to you. I'm thinking of taking over the running of this place, you see? I think it could be run a bit more efficiently. I got a lot of ideas, a lot of plans.

He eyes DAVIES.

How would you like to stay on here, as caretaker?

DAVIES

What?

MICK

I'll be quite open with you. I could rely on a man like
you around the place, keeping an eye on things.

DAVIES

Well now ... wait a minute ... I ... I ain't never done no
caretaking before, you know...

MICK

Doesn't matter about that. It's just that you look a
capable sort of man to me.

DAVIES

I am a capable sort of man. I mean to say, I've had
plenty offers in my time, you know, there's no getting
away from that.

MICK

Well, I could see before, when you took out that knife,
that you wouldn't let anyone mess you about.

DAVIES

No one messes me about, man.

MICK

I mean, you've been in the services, haven't you?

DAVIES

The what?

MICK

You been in the services. You can tell by your stance.

DAVIES

Oh ... yes. Spent half my life there, man. Overseas ...
like ... serving ... I was.

MICK

In the colonies, weren't you?

DAVIES

I was over there. I was one of the first over there.

MICK

That's it. You're just the man I been looking for.

DAVIES

What for?

MICK

Caretaker.

DAVIES

Yes, well ... look ... listen ... who's the landlord here,
him or you?

MICK

Me. I am. I got deeds to prove it.

DAVIES

Ah ...

Decisively.

Well listen, I don't mind doing a bit of caretaking, I
wouldn't mind looking after the place for you.

MICK

Of course, we'd come to a small financial agreement,
mutually beneficial.

DAVIES

I leave you to reckon that out, like.

MICK

Thanks. There's only one thing.

DAVIES

What's that?

MICK

Can you give me any references?

DAVIES

Eh?

MICK

Just to satisfy my solicitor.

DAVIES

I got plenty of references. All I got to do is to go down
to Sidcup tomorrow. I got all the references I want
down there.

MICK

Where's that?

DAVIES

Sidcup. He ain't only got my references down there, he
got all my papers down there. I know that place like the
back of my hand. I'm going down there anyway, see
what I mean, I got to get down there, or I'm done.

MICK

So we can always get hold of these references if we want
them.

DAVIES

I'll be down there any day, I tell you. I was going down
today, but I'm ... I'm waiting for the weather to break.

MICK

Ah.

DAVIES

Listen. You can't pick me up a pair of good shoes, can
you? I got a bad need for a good pair of shoes. I can't
get anywhere without a pair of good shoes, see? Do you
think there's any chance of you being able to pick me up
a pair?

The lights fade to blackout.

Lights up. Morning.

ASTON *is pulling on his trousers over long underwear.*
A slight grimace. He looks around at the head of his
bed, takes a towel from the rail and waves it about. He
pulls it down, goes to DAVIES *and wakes him.* DAVIES
sits up abruptly.

ASTON

You said you wanted me to get you up.

DAVIES

What for?

ASTON

You said you were thinking of going to Sidcup.

DAVIES

Ay, that'd be a good thing, if I got there.

ASTON

Doesn't look much of a day.

DAVIES

Ay, well, that's shot it, en't it?

ASTON

I ... I didn't have a very good night again.

DAVIES

I slept terrible.

Pause.

ASTON

You were making ...

DAVIES

Terrible. Had a bit of rain in the night, didn't it?

ASTON

Just a bit.

He goes to his bed, picks up a small plank and begins to sandpaper it.

DAVIES

Thought so. Come in on my head.

Pause.

Draught's blowing right in on my head, anyway.

Pause.

Can't you close that window behind that sack?

ASTON

You could.

DAVIES

Well then, what about it, then? The rain's coming right in on my head.

ASTON

Got to have a bit of air.

DAVIES *gets out of bed. He is wearing his trousers, waistcoat and vest.*

DAVIES

(*putting on his sandals*) Listen. I've lived all my life in the air, boy. You don't have to tell me about air. What I'm saying is, there's too much air coming in that window when I'm asleep.

ASTON

Gets very stuffy in here without that window open.

ASTON *crosses to the chair, puts the plank on it, and continues sandpapering.*

DAVIES

Yes, but listen, you don't know what I'm telling you. That bloody rain, man, come right in.on my head. Spoils my sleep. I could catch my death of cold with it, with that draught. That's all I'm saying. Just shut that window and no one's going to catch any colds, that's all I'm saying.

Pause.

ASTON

I couldn't sleep in here without that window open.

DAVIES

Yes, but what about me? What ... what you got to say about my position?

ASTON

Why don't you sleep the other way round?

DAVIES

What do you mean?

ASTON

Sleep with your feet to the window.

DAVIES

What good would that do?

ASTON

The rain wouldn't come in on your head.

DAVIES

No, I couldn't do that. I couldn't do that.

Pause.

I mean, I got used to sleeping this way. It isn't me has to change, it's that window. You see, it's raining now. Look at it. It's coming down now.

Pause.

ASTON

I think I'll have a walk down to Goldhawk Road. I got talking to a man there. He had a saw bench. It looked in pretty good condition to me. Don't think it's much good to him.

Pause.

Have a walk down there, I think.

DAVIES

Listen to that. That's done my trip to Sidcup. Eh, what about closing that window now? It'll be coming in here.

ASTON

Close it for the time being.

DAVIES *closes the window and looks out.*

DAVIES

What's all that under that tarpaulin out there?

ASTON

Wood.

DAVIES

What for?

ASTON

To build my shed.

DAVIES *sits on his bed.*

DAVIES

You haven't come across that pair of shoes you was going to look out for me, have you?

ASTON

Oh. No. I'll see if I can pick some up today.

DAVIES

I can't go out in this with these, can I? I can't even go out and get a cup of tea.

ASTON

There's a café just along the road.

DAVIES

There may be, mate.

During ASTON's *speech the room grows darker.*

By the close of the speech only ASTON *can be seen clearly.* DAVIES *and all the other objects are in the shadow. The fade-down of the light must be as gradual, as protracted and as unobtrusive as possible.*

I used to go there quite a bit. Oh, years ago now. But I stopped. I used to like that place. Spent quite a bit of time in there. That was before I went away. Just before. I think that ... place had a lot to do with it. They were all ... a good bit older than me. But they always used to listen. I thought ... they understood what I said. I mean I used to talk to them. I talked too much. That was my mistake. The same in the factory. Standing there, or in the breaks, I used to ... talk about things. And these men, they used to listen, whenever I ... had anything to say. It was all right. The trouble was, I used to have kind of hallucinations. They weren't hallucinations, they ... I used to get the feeling I could see things ... very clearly ... everything ... was so clear ... everything used ... everything used to get very quiet ... everything got very quiet ... all this ... quiet ... and ... this clear sight ... it was ... but maybe I was wrong. Anyway, someone must have said something. I didn't know anything about it. And ... some kind of lie must have got around. And this lie went round. I thought people started being funny. In that café. The factory. I couldn't understand it. Then one day they took me to a hospital, right outside London. They ... got me there. I didn't want to go. Anyway ... I tried to get out, quite a few times. But ... it wasn't very easy. They asked me questions, in there. Got me in and asked me all sorts of questions. Well, I told them ... when they wanted to know ... what my thoughts were. Hmmnn. Then one day ... this man ... doctor, I suppose ... the head one ... he was quite a man of ... distinction ... although I wasn't so sure about that. He called me in. He said ... he told me I had something. He said they'd concluded their examination. That's what he said. And he showed me a pile of papers and he said that I'd got something, some complaint. He said . . . he just said that, you see. You've got . . . this thing. That's your complaint. And we've decided, he said, that in your interests there's only one course we can take. He said . . . but I can't . . . exactly remember . . . how he put it . . . he said, we're going to do something to your brain. He said . . . if we don't, you'll be in here for the rest of your life, but if we do, you stand a chance. You can go out, he said, and live like the others. What do you want to do to my brain, I said to him. But he just repeated what he'd said. Well, I wasn't a fool. I knew I was a minor. I knew he couldn't do anything to me without getting permission. I knew he had to get permission from my mother. So I wrote to her and told her what they were trying to do. But she signed their form, you see, giving them permission. I know that because he showed me her signature when I brought it up. Well, that night I tried to escape, that night. I spent five hours sawing at one of the bars on the window in this ward. Right throughout the dark. They used to shine a torch over the beds every half hour. So I timed it just right. And then it was nearly done, and a man had a . . . he had a fit, right next to me. And they caught me, anyway. About a week later they started to come round and do this thing to the brain. We were all supposed to have it done, in this ward. And they came round and did it one at a time. One a night. I was one of the last. And I could see quite clearly what they did to the others. They used to come round with these . . . I don't know what they were . . . they looked like big pincers, with wires on, the wires were attached to a little machine. It was electric. They used to hold the man down, and this chief ... the chief doctor, used to fit the pincers, something like earphones, he used to fit them on either side of the man's skull. There was a man holding the machine, you see, and he'd ... turn it on, and the chief would just press these pincers on either side of the skull and keep them there. Then he'd take them off. They'd cover the man up ... and they wouldn't touch him again until later on. Some used to put up a fight, but most of them didn't. They just lay there. Well, they were coming round to me, and the night they came I got up and stood against the wall. They told me to get on the bed, and I knew they had to get me on the bed because if they did it while I was standing up they might break my spine. So I stood up and then one or two of them came for me, well, I was younger then, I was much stronger than I am now, I was quite strong then, I laid one of them out and I had another one round the throat, and then suddenly this chief had these pincers on my skull and I knew he wasn't supposed to do it while I was standing up, that's why I ... anyway, he did it. So I did get out. I got out of the place ... but I couldn't walk very well. I don't think my spine was damaged. That was perfectly all right. The trouble was ... my thoughts ... had become very slow ... I couldn't think at all ... I couldn't ... get ... my thoughts ... together ... uuuhh ... I could ... never quite get it ... together. The trouble was, I couldn't hear what people were saying. I couldn't look to the right or the left, I had to look straight in front of me, because if I turned my head round ... I couldn't keep ... upright. And I had these headaches. I used to sit in my room. That was when I lived with my mother. And my brother. He was younger than me. And I laid everything out in order, in my room, all the things I knew were mine, but I didn't die. The thing is, I should have been dead. I should have died. Anyway, I feel much better now. But I don't talk to people now. I steer clear of places like that café. I never go into them now. I don't talk to anyone . . . like that. I've often thought of going back and trying to find the man who did that to me. But I want to do something first. I want to build that shed out in the garden.

Curtain

Act Three

Two weeks later.

MICK *is lying on the floor, down left, his head resting on the rolled carpet, looking up at the ceiling.*

DAVIES *is sitting in the chair, holding his pipe. He is wearing the smoking-jacket. It is afternoon.*

Silence.

DAVIES
I got a feeling he's done something to them cracks.

Pause.

See, there's been plenty of rain in the last week, but it ain't been dripping into the bucket.

Pause.

He must have tarred it over up there.

Pause.

There was someone walking about on the roof the other night. It must have been him.

Pause.

But I got a feeling he's tarred it over on the roof up there. Ain't said a word to me about it. Don't say a word to me.

Pause.

He don't answer me when I talk to him.

He lights a match, holds it to his pipe, and blows it.

He don't give me no knife!

Pause.

He don't give me no knife to cut my bread.

Pause.

How can I cut a loaf of bread without no knife?

Pause.

It's an impossibility.

Pause.

MICK

You've got a knife.

DAVIES

What?

MICK

You've got a knife.

DAVIES

I got a knife, sure I got a knife, but how do you expect me to cut a good loaf of bread with that? That's not a bread-knife. It's nothing to do with cutting bread. I picked it up somewhere. I don't know where it's been, do I? No, what I want –

MICK

I know what you want.

94

Pause. DAVIES *rises and goes to the gas stove.*

What about this gas stove? He tells me it's not connected. How do I know it's not connected? Here I am, I'm sleeping right with it, I wake up in the middle of the night, I'm looking right into the oven, man! It's right next to my face, how do I know, I could be lying there in bed, it might blow up, it might do me harm!

Pause.

But he don't seem to take any notice of what I say to him. I told him the other day, see, I told him about them Blacks, about them Blacks coming up from next door, and using the lavatory. I told him, it was all dirty in there, all the banisters were dirty, they were black, all the lavatory was black. But what did he do? He's supposed to be in charge of it here, he had nothing to say, he hadn't got a word to say.

Pause.

Couple of weeks ago ... he sat there, he give me a long chat ... about a couple of weeks ago. A long chat he give me. Since then he ain't said hardly a word. He went on talking there ... I don't know what he was ... he wasn't looking at me, he wasn't talking to me, he don't care about me. He was talking to himself! That's all he worries about. I mean, you come up to me, you ask my advice, he wouldn't never do a thing like that. I mean, we don't have any conversation, you see? You can't live in the same room with someone who ... who don't have any conversation with you.

Pause.

I just can't get the hang of him.

Pause.

You and me, we could get this place going.

MICK

(*ruminatively*) Yes, you're quite right. Look what I could do with this place.

Pause.

I could turn this place into a penthouse. For instance ... this room. This room you could have as the kitchen. Right size, nice window, sun comes in. I'd have ... I'd have teal-blue, copper and parchment linoleum squares. I'd have those colours re-echoed in the walls. I'd offset the kitchen units with charcoal-grey worktops. Plenty of room for cupboards for the crockery. We'd have a small wall cupboard, a large wall cupboard, a corner wall cupboard with revolving shelves. You wouldn't be short of cupboards. You could put the dining-room across the landing, see? Yes. Venetian blinds on the window, cork floor, cork tiles. You could have an off-white pile linen rug, a table in ... in afromosia teak veneer, sideboard with matt black drawers, curved chairs with cushioned seats, armchairs in oatmeal tweed, a beech frame settee with a woven sea-grass seat, white-topped heat-resistant coffee table, white tile surround. Yes. Then the bedroom. What's a bedroom? It's a retreat. It's a place to go for rest and peace. So you want quiet decoration. The lighting functional. Furniture ... mahogany and rosewood. Deep azure-blue carpet, unglazed blue and white curtains, a bedspread with a pattern of small blue roses on a white ground, dressing-table with a lift-up

96

top containing a plastic tray, table lamp of white raffia . . .

MICK *sits up*.

It wouldn't be a flat it'd be a palace.

DAVIES

I'd say it would, man.

MICK

A palace.

DAVIES

Who would live there?

MICK

I would. My brother and me.

Pause.

DAVIES

What about me?

MICK

(*quietly*) All this junk here, it's no good to anyone. It's just a lot of old iron, that's all. Clobber. You couldn't make a home out of this. There's no way you could arrange it. It's junk. He could never sell it, either, he wouldn't get tuppence for it.

Pause.

Junk.

Pause.

But he doesn't seem to be interested in what I got in mind, that's the trouble. Why don't you have a chat with him, see if he's interested?

97

DAVIES

Me?

MICK

Yes. You're a friend of his.

DAVIES

He's no friend of mine.

MICK

You're living in the same room with him, en't you?

DAVIES

He's no friend of mine. You don't know where you are with him. I mean, with a bloke like you, you know where you are.

MICK *looks at him.*

I mean, you got your own ways, I'm not saying you ain't got your own ways, anyone can see that. You may have some funny ways, but that's the same with all of us, but with him it's different, see? I mean at least with you, the thing with you is you're ...

MICK

Straightforward.

DAVIES

That's it, you're straightforward.

MICK

Yes.

DAVIES

But with him, you don't know what he's up to half the time!

Uh.

He's got no feelings!

Pause.

See, what I need is a clock! I need a clock to tell the time! How can I tell the time without a clock? I can't do it! I said to him, I said, look here, what about getting in a clock, so's I can tell what time it is? I mean, if you can't tell what time you're at you don't know where you are, you understand my meaning? See, what I got to do now, if I'm walking about outside, I got to get my eye on a clock, and keep the time in my head for when I come in. But that's no good, I mean I'm not in here five minutes and I forgotten it. I forgotten what time it was!

DAVIES *walks up and down the room.*

Look at it this way. If I don't feel well I have a bit of a lay down, then, when I wake up, I don't know what time it is to go and have a cup of tea! You see, it's not so bad when I'm coming in. I can see the clock on the corner, the moment I'm stepping into the house I know what the time is, but when I'm *in*! It's when I'm *in* … that I haven't the foggiest idea what time it is!

Pause.

No, what I need is a clock in here, in this room, and then I stand a bit of a chance. But he don't give me one.

DAVIES *sits in the chair.*

He wakes me up! He wakes me up in the middle of the

night! Tells me I'm making noises! I tell you I've half a mind to give him a mouthful one of these days.

MICK

He don't let you sleep?

DAVIES

He don't let me sleep! He wakes me up!

MICK

That's terrible.

DAVIES

I been plenty of other places. They always let me sleep. It's the same the whole world over. Except here.

MICK

Sleep's essential. I've always said that.

DAVIES

You're right, it's essential. I get up in the morning, I'm worn out! I got business to see to. I got to move myself, I got to sort myself out, I got to get fixed up. But when I wake up in the morning, I ain't got no energy in me. And on top of that I ain't got no clock.

MICK

Yes.

DAVIES

(*standing, moving*) He goes out, I don't know where he goes to, where's he go, he never tells me. We used to have a bit of a chat, not any more. I never see him, he goes out, he comes in late, next thing I know he's shoving me about in the middle of the night.

Pause.

Listen! I wake up in the morning ... I wake up in the morning and he's smiling at me! He's standing there, looking at me, smiling! I can see him, you see, I can see him through the blanket. He puts on his coat, he turns himself round, he looks down at my bed, there's a smile on his face! What the hell's he smiling at? What he don't know is that I'm watching him through that blanket. He don't know that! He don't know I can see him, he thinks I'm asleep, but I got my eye on him all the time through the blanket, see? But he don't know that! He just looks at me and he smiles, but he don't know that I can see him doing it!

Pause.

Bending, close to MICK.

No, what you want to do, you want to speak to him, see? I got ... I got that worked out. You want to tell him ... that we got ideas for this place, we could build it up, we could get it started. You see, I could decorate it out for you, I could give you a hand in doing it ... between us.

Pause.

Where do you live now, then?

MICK

Me? Oh, I've got a little place. Not bad. Everything laid on. You must come up and have a drink some time. Listen to some Tchaikovsky.

DAVIES

No, you see, you're the bloke who wants to talk to him. I mean, you're his brother.

Pause.

MICK

Yes ... maybe I will.

A door bangs.

MICK *rises, goes to the door and exits.*

DAVIES

Where you going? This is him!

Silence.

DAVIES *stands, then goes to the window and looks out.*

ASTON *enters. He is carrying a paper bag. He takes off his overcoat, opens the bag and takes out a pair of shoes.*

ASTON

Pair of shoes.

DAVIES

(*turning*) What?

ASTON

I picked them up. Try them.

DAVIES

Shoes? What sort?

ASTON

They might do you.

DAVIES *comes down stage, takes off his sandals and tries the shoes on. He walks about, waggling his feet, bends, and presses the leather.*

DAVIES

No, they're not right.

ASTON

Aren't they?

DAVIES

No, they don't fit.

ASTON

Mmnn.

Pause.

DAVIES

Well, I'll tell you what, they might do ... until I get
another pair.

Pause.

Where's the laces?

ASTON

No laces.

DAVIES

I can't wear them without laces.

ASTON

I just got the shoes.

DAVIES

Well now, look that puts the lid on it, don't it? I mean,
you couldn't keep these shoes on right without a pair of
laces. The only way to keep a pair of shoes on, if you
haven't got no laces, is to tighten the foot, see? Walk
about with a tight foot, see? Well, that's no good for the
foot. Puts a bad strain on the foot. If you can do the

shoes up proper there's less chance of you getting a strain.

ASTON *goes round to the top of his bed.*

ASTON

I might have some somewhere.

DAVIES

You see what I'm getting at?

Pause.

ASTON

Here's some.

He hands them to DAVIES.

DAVIES

These are brown.

ASTON

That's all I got.

DAVIES

These shoes are black.

ASTON *does not answer.*

Well, they can do, anyway, until I get another pair.

DAVIES *sits in the chair and begins to lace his shoes.*

Maybe they'll get me down to Sidcup tomorrow. If I get down there I'll be able to sort myself out.

Pause.

I've been offered a good job. Man has offered it to me, he's . . . he's got plenty of ideas. He's got a bit of a future. But they want my papers, you see, they want my references. I'd have to get down to Sidcup before I could get hold of them. That's where they are, see. Trouble is, getting there. That's my problem. The weather's dead against it.

ASTON *quietly exits, unnoticed.*

Don't know as these shoes'll be much good. It's a hard road, I been down there before. Coming the other way, like. Last time I left there, it was ... last time ... getting on a while back ... the road was bad, the rain was coming down, lucky I didn't die there on the road, but I got here, I kept going, all along ... yes ... I kept going all along. But all the same, I can't go on like this, what I got to do, I got to get back there, find this man –

He turns and looks about the room.

Christ! That bastard, he ain't even listening to me!

Blackout.

DIM LIGHT THROUGH THE WINDOW.

It is night. ASTON *and* DAVIES *are in bed,* DAVIES *groaning.*

ASTON *sits up, gets out of bed, switches on the light, goes over to* DAVIES *and shakes him.*

ASTON
Hey, stop it, will you? I can't sleep.

DAVIES
What? What? What's going on?

ASTON

You're making noises.

DAVIES

I'm an old man, what do you expect me to do, stop
breathing?

ASTON

You're making noises.

DAVIES

What do you expect me to do, stop breathing?

ASTON *goes to his bed, and puts on his trousers.*

ASTON

I'll get a bit of air.

DAVIES

What do you expect me to do? I tell you mate, I'm not
surprised they took you in. Waking an old man up in
the middle of the night, you must be off your nut!
Giving me bad dreams, who's responsible, then, for me
having bad dreams? If you wouldn't keep mucking me
about I wouldn't make no noises! How do you expect
me to sleep peaceful when you keep poking me all the
time? What do you want me to do, stop breathing?

*He throws the cover off and gets out of bed, wearing his
vest, waistcoat and trousers.*

It's getting so freezing in here I have to keep my trousers
on to go to bed. I never done that before in my life. But
that's what I got to do here. Just because you won't put
in any bleeding heating! I've had just about enough with
you mucking me about. I've seen better days than you
have, man. Nobody ever got me inside one of them

places, anyway. I'm a sane man! So don't you start mucking me about. I'll be all right as long as you keep your place. Just you keep your place, that's all. Because I can tell you, your brother's got his eye on you. He knows all about you. I got a friend there, don't you worry about that. I got a true pal there. Treating me like dirt! Why'd you invite me in here in the first place if you was going to treat me like this? You think you're better than me you got another think coming. I know enough. They had you inside one of them places before, they can have you inside again. Your brother's got his eye on you! They can put the pincers on your head again, man! They can have them on again! Any time. All they got to do is get the word. They'd carry you in there, boy. They'd come here and pick you up and carry you in! They'd keep you fixed! They'd put them pincers on your head, they'd have you fixed! They'd take one look at all this junk I got to sleep with they'd know you were a creamer. That was the greatest mistake they made, you take my tip, letting you get out of that place. Nobody knows what you're at, you go out you come in, nobody knows what you're at! Well, nobody messes me about for long. You think I'm going to do your dirty work? Haaaaahhhhh! You better think again! You want me to do all the dirty work all up and down them stairs just so I can sleep in this lousy filthy hole every night? Not me, boy. Not for you boy. You don't know what you're doing half the time. You're up the creek! You're half off! You can tell it by looking at you. Who ever saw you slip me a few bob? Treating me like a bloody animal! I never been inside a nuthouse!

ASTON *makes a slight move towards him.* DAVIES *takes his knife from his back pocket.*

Don't come nothing with me, mate. I got this here. I used it. I used it. Don't come it with me.

A pause. They stare at each other.

Mind what you do now.

Pause.

Don't you try anything with me.

Pause.

ASTON

I ... I think it's about time you found somewhere else. I don't think we're hitting it off.

DAVIES

Find somewhere else?

ASTON

Yes.

DAVIES

Me? You talking to me? Not me, man! You!

ASTON

What?

DAVIES

You! You better find somewhere else!

ASTON

I live here. You don't.

DAVIES

Don't I? Well, I live here. I been offered a job here.

ASTON

Yes ... well, I don't think you're really suitable.

DAVIES

Not suitable? Well, I can tell you, there's someone here thinks I am suitable. And I'll tell you. I'm staying on here as caretaker! Get it! Your brother, he's told me, see, he's told me the job is mine. Mine! So that's where I am. I'm going to be his caretaker.

ASTON

My brother?

DAVIES

He's staying, he's going to run this place, and I'm staying with him.

ASTON

Look. If I give you ... a few bob you can get down to Sidcup.

DAVIES

You build your shed first! A few bob! When I can earn a steady wage here! You build your stinking shed first! That's what!

ASTON *stares at him.*

ASTON

That's not a stinking shed.

Silence.

ASTON *moves to him.*

It's clean. It's all good wood. I'll get it up. No trouble.

DAVIES

Don't you come too near!

ASTON

You've no reason to call that shed stinking.

DAVIES *points the knife.*

You stink.

DAVIES

What!

ASTON

You've been stinking the place out.

DAVIES

Christ, you say that to me!

ASTON

For days. That's one reason I can't sleep.

DAVIES

You call me that! You call me stinking!

ASTON

You better go.

DAVIES

I'll stink you!

*He thrusts his arm out, the arm trembling, the knife
pointing at* ASTON's *stomach.* ASTON *does not move.
Silence.* DAVIES' *arm moves no further. They stand.*

I'll stink you . . .

Pause.

ASTON

Get your stuff.

DAVIES *draws the knife in to his chest, breathing*

heavily. ASTON *goes to* DAVIES' *bed, collects his bag and puts a few of* DAVIES' *things into it.*

DAVIES

You ain't ... you ain't got the right ... Leave that alone, that's mine!

DAVIES *takes the bag and presses the contents down.*

All right ... I been offered a job here ... you wait ...

He puts on his smoking-jacket.

... you wait ... your brother ... he'll sort you out ... you call me that ... you call me that ... no one's ever called me that ...

He puts on his overcoat.

You'll be sorry you called me that ... you ain't heard the last of this ...

He picks up his bag and goes to the door.

You'll be sorry you called me that ...

He opens the door, ASTON *watching him.*

Now I know who I can trust.

DAVIES *goes out.* ASTON *stands.*

Blackout.

Lights up. Early evening.

Voices on the stairs.

MICK *and* DAVIES *enter.*

DAVIES

Stink! You hear that! Me! I told you what he said,
didn't I? Stink! You hear that? That's what he said to
me!

MICK

Tch, tch, tch.

DAVIES

That's what he said to me.

MICK

You don't stink.

DAVIES

No, sir!

MICK

If you stank I'd be the first one to tell you.

DAVIES

I told him, I told him he . . . I said to him, you ain't
heard the last of this, man! I said, don't you forget your
brother. I told him you'd be coming along to sort him
out. He don't know what he's started, doing that. Doing
that to me. I said to him, I said to him, he'll be along,
your brother'll be along, he's got sense, not like you –

MICK

What do you mean?

DAVIES

Eh?

MICK

You saying my brother hasn't got any sense?

What? What I'm saying is, you got ideas for this place,
all this ... all this decorating, see? I mean, he's got no
right to order me about. I take orders from you, I do my
caretaking for you, I mean, you look upon me ... you
don't treat me like a lump of dirt ... we can both ... we
can both see him for what he is.

Pause.

MICK

What did he say then, when you told him I'd offered
you the job as caretaker?

DAVIES

He ... he said ... he said ... something about ... he
lived here.

MICK

Yes, he's got a point, en he?

DAVIES

A point! This is your house, en't? You let him live here!

MICK

I could tell him to go, I suppose.

DAVIES

That's what I'm saying.

MICK

Yes. I could tell him to go. I mean, I'm the landlord. On
the other hand, he's the sitting tenant. Giving him
notice, you see, what it is, it's a technical matter, that's
what it is. It depends how you regard this room. I mean
it depends whether you regard this room as furnished or
unfurnished. See what I mean?

DAVIES

No, I don't.

MICK

All this furniture, you see, in here, it's all his, except the beds, of course. So what it is, it's a fine legal point, that's what it is.

Pause.

DAVIES

I tell you he should go back where he come from!

MICK

(*turning to look at him*) Come from?

DAVIES

Yes.

MICK

Where did he come from?

DAVIES

Well ... he ... he ...

MICK

You get a bit out of your depth sometimes, don't you?

Pause.

(*rising, briskly*) Well, anyway, as things stand, I don't mind having a go at doing up the place ...

DAVIES

That's what I wanted to hear!

MICK

No, I don't mind.

He turns to face DAVIES.

But you better be as good as you say you are.

DAVIES

What do you mean?

MICK

Well, you say you're an interior decorator, you'd better
be a good one.

DAVIES

A what?

MICK

What do you mean, a what? A decorator. An interior
decorator.

DAVIES

Me? What do you mean? I never touched that. I never
been that.

MICK

You've never what?

DAVIES

No, no, not me, man. I'm not an interior decorator. I
been too busy. Too many other things to do, you see.
But I ... but I could always turn my hand to most
things ... give me ... give me a bit of time to pick it up.

MICK

I don't want you to pick it up. I want a first-class
experienced interior decorator. I thought you were one.

DAVIES

Me? Now wait a minute – wait a minute – you got the
wrong man.

MICK

How could I have the wrong man? You're the only man
I've spoken to. You're the only man I've told, about my
dreams, about my deepest wishes, you're the only one
I've told, and I only told you because I understood you
were an experienced first-class professional interior and
exterior decorator.

DAVIES

Now look here –

MICK

You mean you wouldn't know how to fit teal-blue,
copper and parchment linoleum squares and have those
colours re-echoed in the walls?

DAVIES

Now, look here, where'd you get – ?

MICK

You wouldn't be able to decorate out a table in
afromosia teak veneer, an armchair in oatmeal tweed
and a beech frame settee with a woven sea-grass seat?

DAVIES

I never said that!

MICK

Christ! I must have been under a false impression!

DAVIES

I never said it!

MICK

You're a bloody imposter, mate!

Now you don't want to say that sort of thing to me.
You took me on here as caretaker. I was going to give
you a helping hand, that's all, for a small ... for a small
wage, I never said nothing about that ... you start
calling me names –

MICK

What is your name?

DAVIES

Don't start that –

MICK

No, what's your real name?

DAVIES

My real name's Davies.

MICK

What's the name you go under?

DAVIES

Jenkins!

MICK

You got two names. What about the rest? Eh? Now
come on, why did you tell me all this dirt about you
being an interior decorator?

DAVIES

I didn't tell you nothing! Won't you listen to what I'm
saying?

Pause.

It was him who told you. It was your brother who must
have told you. He's nutty! He'd tell you anything, out of

spite, he's nutty, he's half way gone, it was him who told you.

MICK *walks slowly to him.*

MICK
What did you call my brother?

DAVIES
When?

MICK
He's what?

DAVIES
I ... now get this straight ...

MICK
Nutty? Who's nutty?

Pause.

Did you call my brother nutty? My brother. That's a bit of ... that's a bit of an impertinent thing to say, isn't it?

DAVIES
But he says so himself!

MICK *walks slowly round* DAVIES' *figure, regarding him, once.*

MICK
What a strange man you are. Aren't you? You're really strange. Ever since you come into this house there's been nothing but trouble. Honest. I can take nothing you say at face value. Every word you speak is open to any number of different interpretations. Most of what you say is lies. You're violent, you're erratic, you're just

completely unpredictable. You're nothing else but a wild animal, when you come down to it. You're a barbarian. And to put the old tin lid on it, you stink from arse-hole to breakfast time. Look at it. You come here recommending yourself as an interior decorator, whereupon I take you on, and what happens? You make a long speech about all the references you've got down at Sidcup, and what happens? I haven't noticed you go down to Sidcup to obtain them. It's all most regrettable but it looks as though I'm compelled to pay you off for your caretaking work. Here's half a dollar.

He feels in his pocket, takes out a half-crown and tosses it at DAVIES' *feet.* DAVIES *stands still.* MICK *walks to the gas stove and picks up the Buddha.*

DAVIES

(*slowly*) All right then ... you do that ... you do it ... if that's what you want ...

MICK

THAT'S WHAT I WANT!

He hurls the Buddha against the gas stove. It breaks.

(*passionately*) Anyone would think this house was all I got to worry about. I got plenty of other things I can worry about. I've got other things. I've got plenty of other interests. I've got my own business to build up, haven't I? I got to think about expanding ... in all directions. I don't stand still. I'm moving about, all the time. I'm moving ... all the time. I've got to think about the future. I'm not worried about this house. I'm not interested. My brother can worry about it. He can do it up, he can decorate it, he can do what he likes with it.

I'm not bothered. I thought I was doing him a favour, letting him live here. He's got his own ideas. Let him have them. I'm going to chuck it in.

Pause.

DAVIES

What about me?

Silence. MICK *does not look at him.*

A door bangs.

Silence. They do not move.

ASTON *comes in. He closes the door, moves into the room and faces* MICK. *They look at each other. Both are smiling, faintly.*

MICK

(*beginning to speak to* ASTON) Look ... uh ...

He stops, goes to the door and exits. ASTON *leaves the door open, crosses behind* DAVIES, *sees the broken Buddha, and looks at the pieces for a moment. He then goes to his bed, takes off his overcoat, sits, takes the screwdriver and plug and pokes the plug.*

DAVIES

I just come back for my pipe.

ASTON

Oh yes.

DAVIES

I got out and ... half way down I ... I suddenly ... found out ... you see ... that I hadn't got my pipe. So I come back to get it ...

Pause. He moves to ASTON.

That ain't the same plug, is it, you been ...?

Pause.

Still can't get anywhere with it, eh?

Pause.

Well, if you ... persevere, in my opinion, you'll
probably ...

Pause.

Listen ...

Pause.

You didn't mean that, did you, about me stinking, did
you?

Pause.

Did you? You been a good friend to me. You took me
in. You took me in, you didn't ask me no questions, you
give me a bed, you been a mate to me. Listen. I been
thinking, why I made all them noises, it was because of
the draught, see, that draught was on me as I was
sleeping, made me make noises without me knowing it,
so I been thinking, what I mean to say, if you was to
give me your bed, and you have my bed, there's not all
that difference between them, they're the same sort of
bed, if I was to have yourn, you sleep, wherever bed
you're in, so you have mine, I have yourn, and that'll be
all right, I'll be out of the draught, see, I mean, you
don't mind a bit of wind, you need a bit of air, I can
understand that, you being in that place that time, with

all them doctors and all they done, closed up, I know them places, too hot, you see, they're always too hot, I had a peep in one once, nearly suffocated me, so I reckon that'd be the best way out of it, we swap beds, and then we could get down to what we was saying, I'd look after the place for you, I'd keep an eye on it for you, for you, like, not for the other ... not for ... for your brother, you see, not for him, for you, I'll be your man, you say the word, just say the word ...

Pause.

What do you think of this I'm saying?

Pause.

ASTON

No, I like sleeping in this bed.

DAVIES

But you don't understand my meaning!

ASTON

Anyway, that one's my brother's bed.

DAVIES

Your brother?

ASTON

Any time he stays here. This is my bed. It's the only bed I can sleep in.

DAVIES

But your brother's gone! He's gone!

Pause.

ASTON

No. I couldn't change beds.

DAVIES

But you don't understand my meaning!

ASTON

Anyway, I'm going to be busy. I've got that shed to get
up. If I don't get it up now it'll never go up. Until it's up
I can't get started.

DAVIES

I'll give you a hand to put up your shed, that's what I'll
do!

Pause.

I'll give you a hand! We'll both put up that shed
together! See? Get it done in next to no time! Do you
see what I'm saying?

Pause.

ASTON

No. I can get it up myself.

DAVIES

But listen. I'm with you, I'll be here, I'll do it for you!

Pause.

We'll do it together!

Pause.

Christ, we'll change beds!

ASTON *moves to the window and stands with his back
to* DAVIES.

You mean you're throwing me out? You can't do that. Listen man, listen man, I don't mind, you see, I don't mind, I'll stay, I don't mind, I'll tell you what, if you don't want to change beds, we'll keep it as it is, I'll stay in the same bed, maybe if I can get a stronger piece of sacking, like, to go over the window, keep out the draught, that'll do it, what do you say, we'll keep it as it is?

Pause.

ASTON

No.

DAVIES

Why ... not?

ASTON *turns to look at him.*

ASTON

You make too much noise.

DAVIES

But ... but ... look ... listen ... listen here ... I mean ...

ASTON *turns back to the window.*

What am I going to do?

Pause.

What shall I do?

Pause.

Where am I going to go?

Pause.

If you want me to go ... I'll go. You just say the word.

Pause.

I'll tell you what though ... them shoes ... them shoes you give me ... they're working out all right ... they're all right. Maybe I could ... get down ...

ASTON *remains still, his back to him, at the window.*

Listen ... if I ... got down ... if I was to ... get my papers ... would you ... would you let ... would you ... if I got down ... and got my ...

Long silence.

Curtain.